Marth

W9-BSB-149

**Praise for**
*Moving Toward the Millionth Circle*

"No one has done more than Jean Shinoda Bolen to awaken the global heart. With *Moving Toward the Millionth Circle,* she continues to inspire and direct the spiritual uprising of women around the world."

—Marianne Williamson

"I believe that heart-centered feminine activism can change the world, and I agree with Jean Bolen that now is the time to do it. In her book, she describes how every woman can be supported by a circle of friends with a sacred center, and how circles multiply their spiritual and political energy toward a tipping point."

—Isabel Allende

"My personal tribute to Dr. Bolen for highlighting the need for implementing the UN Security Council resolution 1325 adopted in 2000 which recognizes how women would contribute to peace and security. I wish a wider readership and deeper absorption of the wonderful contents of her book. Dr. Jean Shinoda Bolen has contributed substantively to the ever-increasing focus of recent years on women's empowerment and equality and the importance of their participation at all decision-making levels. Her rich personal experience, perception, and perspective have made the book truly engaging."

—Ambassador Anwarul K. Chowdhury,
Former Under-Secretary General
of the United Nations

MOVING TOWARD

THE MILLIONTH CIRCLE

OTHER BOOKS BY JEAN SHINODA BOLEN, M.D.

*The Tao of Psychology*

*Goddesses in Everywoman*

*Gods in Everyman*

*Ring of Power*

*Crossing to Avalon*

*Close to the Bone*

*The Millionth Circle*

*Goddesses in Older Women*

*Crones Don't Whine*

*Urgent Message From Mother*

*Like a Tree*

# MOVING TOWARD THE MILLIONTH CIRCLE

*Energizing the Global Women's Movement*

ADVOCATING A GLOBAL CONFERENCE ON WOMEN

**JEAN SHINODA BOLEN**, M.D.

Conari Press

First published in 2013 by Conari Press,
an imprint of Red Wheel/Weiser, LLC
With offices at:
665 Third Street, Suite 400
San Francisco, CA 94107
*www.redwheelweiser.com*

Copyright © 2013 by Jean Shinoda Bolen, M.D.
All rights reserved. No part of this publication may be reproduced
or transmitted in any form or by any means, electronic or mechani-
cal, including photocopying, recording, or by any information stor-
age and retrieval system, without permission in writing from Red
Wheel/Weiser, LLC. Reviewers may quote brief passages.

ISBN: 978-1-57324-628-6

Library of Congress Cataloging-in-Publication Data
available upon request

Cover design by Jim Warner
Cover photograph: Yellow Leaf Circle © Martin Hill
Interior by Jane Hagaman
Typeset in Minion and Trajan

Printed in the United States of America
MAL

10  9  8  7  6  5  4  3  2  1

The paper used in this publication meets the minimum requirements of
the American National Standard for Information Sciences—Permanence of
Paper for Printed Library Materials Z39.48-1992 (R1997).

# CONTENTS

*I think the Cherokee approach to life is being able*
*to continually move forward with kind of a good mind*
*and not focus on the negative things in your life*
*and the negative things you see around you,*
*but focus on the positive things and try to look*
*at the larger picture and keep moving forward.*

—Wilma Mankiller, the first woman chief
of the Cherokee Nation

# PREMISE

*The eyes of the future are looking back at us and they are praying for us to see beyond our own time.*

—Terry Tempest Williams

# PREMISE

I THINK OF *Moving Toward the Millionth Circle* as a sequel to *The Millionth Circle* (1999) but with a different focus. *The Millionth Circle* was a guide on how to create and sustain women's circles with a sacred center, which I called "Zen and the Art of Circle Maintenance." It proposed nothing short of bringing humanity into a post-patriarchal era via the proliferation of women's circles through a principle that can be intuitively grasped: when a critical number of people change how they think and behave, the culture does also and a new era begins. The "millionth circle" is a metaphoric number for the tipping point. This second small book was inspired by being at the United Nations during meetings of the Commission on the Status of Women each spring where several thousand activists from grassroots non-governmental organizations (NGOs) that help women and girls present panels and workshops, sharing information and meeting each other. I realized how their effectiveness and numbers would grow exponentially through a world conference on women, and how circles with a sacred center would support women who work for change in their lives and in the world. I became an advocate for a UN conference, not as a goal in itself, but as a huge step toward reaching the tipping point.

*Moving Toward the Millionth Circle* is especially meant for heart-centered activists who are motivated to act by compassionate action, a sense of sisterhood, or fierce mother-bear protectiveness which is a combination of love and outrage. It is for women wherever they are, who are activists because of a promise made to others, to divinity, or to themselves. It may have been a calling or is the result of one step leading to another. It may be a vow to stop a multi-generational pattern of family or institutional or political indifference toward abuse or injustice. It may be a deep conviction that this is yours to do. Activism is a personal choice. It is a passion for a cause expressed through actions, funding, communication, as well as prayer, rituals, and art.

I have been a persevering advocate for a UN 5th World Conference on Women and women's circles because I see the potential for transformative change when women come together in common cause. A world conference would energize a global women's movement by raising consciousness about *what needs doing and can be done once political will is mobilized*: implementing the Beijing Platform for Action and Security Council Resolution 1325 about women, peace, and security are examples. The vision of a world in which women's rights and human rights are one and the same needs to be kept alive, which a global conference would do.

I hope my words will reach younger women who want to get involved in the millionth circle vision and that when there is global conference that they will come and support others to be there. I see possibilities for inter-generational, international mentoring at this conference as a two-way experience that will give to both and change the world. In the late 1960s, consciousness-raising groups formed in the United States and appeared to be just women talking to each other about patriarchy and equality. They validated each other's reality and potential for action. They took their perceptions seriously and with support from their sister-activists whom they did not want to let down, individually and in groups took actions that added up to make history. These circles were the basis of the Women's Movement that changed the world for American women in the 1970s and led to four UN World Conferences on Women between 1975 and 1995.

I am convinced that we can contribute by what we do to how history will turn out. I believe that empowered women in sufficient numbers can truly influence the course of humanity at this time in history and fulfill Nobel Peace Prize recipient Aung San Sun Kyi's vision about the ability of women to contribute to peace. She was under house arrest for fifteof twenty-one years between 1989 and 2010 for her opposition to the military junta's seizure of the democratic government of Burma. In her opening keynote via videotape to the 1995 NGO Forum on Women at the Fourth UN World Conference on Women in Beijing, she said:

> For millennia women have dedicated themselves almost exclusively to the task of nurturing, protecting and caring for the young and the old, striving for the conditions of peace that favour life as a whole . . . Now that we are gaining control of the primary historical role imposed on us of sustaining life in the context of the home and family, it is time to apply in the arena of the world the wisdom and experience thus gained in activities of peace over so many thousands of years. The education and empowerment of women throughout the world cannot fail to result in a more caring, tolerant, just and peaceful life for all.

Grassroots efforts to mobilize support for a World Conference on Women gained the support of the two most important leaders of the United Nations. On March 8, 2012, the Secretary-General Ban Ki-moon and the 66th General Assembly President Nassir Abdulaziz Al-Nasser announced their support in a joint statement. They said "it is high time for a global women's conference, all the more important because of the enormous changes the world is going through, with both positive and other implications for women." They noted the enthusiasm of civil society, particularly women's organizations, for such a conference had added extra strength to their support. It seemed likely that they were responding to the Fifth World Conference for Women Campaign. The symbol "5WCW" on big blue buttons was worn by supporters at the UN and displayed on websites and newsletters. The petition for the conference had over fifteen thousand signatures when they made their joint proposal to have a global women's conference.

The Secretary General and President of the General Assembly asked for member states to submit and pass a draft resolution for a world conference on women in 2015, which would have happened if ambassadors in the General Assembly had responded favorably. They did not.

When "why not?" is asked, the bland and true answer is that "it was not the right time" for this proposal. Later developments suggest support for a global women's conference with UN auspices might be forthcoming if a conference were held without the simultaneous meeting of the member states. The reasons why not were complex, speculative, and based on hearsay and confidential conversations. However, since "why not?" is the very first response by everyone who learns of this, I did want to share my perspective. In the General Assembly, most resolutions are passed by consensus. There was lobbying against the proposal by ambassadors from member states that are against reproductive rights and equality for women. There was displeasure that there had not been consultation before the joint statement was made. Some major NGOs were very concerned about the potential danger to the strong existing UN position on women embodied in the Beijing Platform for Action, and they let this be known. When support from the United States and European Union was not forthcoming, support from countries that initially indicated that they supported the proposal faded.

The idea of a UN global women's conference got a huge boost, however. The possibility had gone from "Forget it, the time of women's conferences is over" to being a hot topic.

The Fourth World Conference on Women, known as the Beijing Conference, was in two parts: the official meeting with representatives from the member states (currently 193 countries) and the NGO Forum, attended by all the others—people from organizations and individuals concerned with women and girls (non-governmental organizations, civil society). Of the forty thousand people who attended, over 90 percent participated in the forum that was, for many, a life-changing experience which then rippled out through their organizations and through what they have since done in the world. The stories I have heard of the effects on the girls and women who went to any of the four UN women's world conferences is what inspires me most about the potential for a 21st century World Conference on Women, which could easily not only draw twice as many people, but also through media, technology, and connections through circles reach millions more. Ideas from such a conference could go viral. The result can be a global women's movement that would accelerate reaching the tipping point.

UN Women (the United Nations Entity for Gender Equality and the Empowerment of Women) was established at the UN in July 2010. There was no such organization when the first four conferences were held. UN entities such as UNICEF (children) and WHO (health) sponsor or co-sponsor international summits and conferences without the 193 member states meeting simultaneously. Support from philanthropy, from individuals and foundations, and from various governments is required to not just hold a conference, but also to provide grants to individual women from organizations in developing countries who do much on the ground but would not have funds to send members to an international meeting. Yet these are the women who inspire and do much with the support that we can provide, and whose reports most touch outrage and hearts to stop the exploitation and abuse of girls and women.

Our first buttons and website used "5WWC" for Fifth Women's World Conference back in 2003 (see the current *5wcw.org* and the archival site *5wwc.org*). We changed to 5WCW when it seemed that this was the only form possible, but now that UN Women exists, there may be a way to have it under UN auspices but without the same structure as in Beijing. Since women from many developing countries may not be able attend unless it is endorsed by the UN, this is important. And if, as we were told, "5WCW" is now a red flag because it connotes member state participation, we may return to "5WWC" or drop it. The intention is to not lose what the button-logo stands for: a grassroots movement to have a global women's conference.

It has been made absolutely clear that women need to become activists on their own behalf. This was the conclusion reached by the largest global study on violence against women (*American Political Science Review*, Weldon, S.L. & Hun, M. Cambridge University Press, 2012). Only strong feminist movements are able to voice and organize around their top priorities as women. This study found astonishingly high rates of sexual assault, stalking, trafficking, and violence in intimate relationships, as well as other violations of women's bodies and psyches. The study included every region of the world, varying degrees of democracy, rich and poor countries, and a variety of the world's religions. It covered 85 percent of the world's population. Without strong feminist movements, abuse of women is sidelined, subordinated to men's needs or to the priorities of institutions or political parties.

Now is the time for circles instead of hierarchies, for people to meet together in a form in which everyone is equal, in person and in virtual online circles. Circles with a sacred center support those in them to be true to themselves, to follow whatever the calling or assignment might be, to support each other, make wise choices, and call upon invisible help through prayers, intentions, and meditation. *Moving Toward the Millionth Circle* is about circles and about heart-centered activists. It is about seeding circles and a global feminist movement. It is about spiritual equality and the healing power of the sacred feminine.

# 2
# HEART-CENTERED ACTIVISM

*What would I do today if I were brave?*
*What if we all meant to do what we secretly dream?*
*If I refused to listen to the voice of fear?*
*and listened to the voice of courage whispering in my ear?*
*And never lose faith even when losing my way?*

—Jana Stanfield

# HEART-CENTERED ACTIVISM

ANY WOMAN WHO realizes the potential of being in a women's circle that can support and sustain the women in them to be true to themselves—and who carries the intention through to midwife a new circle, adds one more toward the metaphoric "millionth circle," that one that tips the culture from patriarchal toward egalitarian, from hierarchy toward collaboration, and from dominance toward interdependence. Truly an epic intention.

Each new circle draws from and adds its energy to the morphic or archetypal field of the circle. The more circles there are the easier and faster it is for new circles with a sacred center to form.

Each established circle that considers itself part of the movement toward the millionth circle, that aligns itself *each time it meets* with this as a conscious intention, adds energy to the field and reminds its members that they are part of a quiet yet evolutionary effort.

It's sacred feminine feminism, or simply *heart-centered activism* to be doing work in the world, community, or family on behalf of women and girls, for the principle of equality, or as an advocate for what is true for you. I believe every activist needs the nourishment that a circle of women can provide to keep on keeping on.

## Heart-Centered Activism

It takes work to be an activist of any kind.

There are twists and turns,

setbacks, large and small victories.

always much to be done

and more to do.

If you are called to be an activist

"take heart" applies.

○

It will be a labyrinthine journey that will test you.

Sometimes it will seem that the path is going straight to the goal,

and then it turns sharply and you feel back to square one,

as in a board game.

Will you give up or will you keep on?

○

Circumstances change, people you counted on

may not come through.

May join forces with others, abandon ship.

Or just run out of steam.

○

It helps all concerned to be in a circle of support

with shared meaning at the center.

Activism is really not a job for a do-it-yourself action hero

even if it depends on one person doing her job

at a particular moment.

When activism is your assignment in the way that I define it,

meaningful, fun, motivated by love,

then it also is soul work.

## Assignments

The idea of recognizing an assignment when one comes along grows through personal encounters with people whose lives and "assignments" are congruent, authentic, and involved in service. There are many, many good causes to become involved with, but the assignment about which I write is one that has your name on it, written so only you know that *this one is for you*. It is something you volunteer to do. Taking on an assignment is an aspect of individuation—of becoming authentically oneself, of being on a path with heart or on a chosen life path. It is doing soul work. And as many may tell you who began with something small but significant, one step leads to another.

The idea that an "assignment" could be your soul work begins with a premise that we have a soul as most everyone throughout time has assumed; if so, there must be some point in being here. An immortal soul comes in through the body of a biological mother, into a world of family, society, culture, and time, that is either welcoming or not. I remember the series of insights that led me to think that we are "spiritual beings on a human path, rather than human beings who may or may not be on a spiritual path" as I wrote in *Close to the Bone: Life-Threatening Illness as a Soul Journey.* Our lives are short, time passes quickly, and we will have our share of suffering and joy. Time, place, skin color, and gender will greatly affect the expectations, opportunities, and limitations placed on us. And yet, if we have a soul, then what we do here in the time we have matters.

In this particular historical and cosmological time, the excesses of alpha male psychology and patriarchy has brought humanity and the planet to the brink, and some of the wiser men look to women to save the situation: "We men have made a proper mess of things, it's up to women to save us," said Desmond Tutu, former Anglican archbishop and Nobel Peace Laureate, or as the nineteenth-century philosopher Matthew Arnold foresaw, "If ever the women of the world came together solely for the benefit of mankind, it would be a force the world has never seen."

I took on the assignment of advocacy for a UN Fifth World Conference on Women (5WCW) as a direct outgrowth of the idea behind the meta-phoric millionth circle. My advocacy was not a goal in itself, but a giant step toward reaching the millionth circle—just as smaller conferences of women and gatherings with this intention also will be. Circles that form during a workshop, as well as ones I have been in for many years, continue to inspire me. I can say from my own experience that "Each circle supports each woman in it to believe in herself and live authentically, to be who she could be with support from the circle and spiritual energy from her deepest sources, and to live into her assignment."

*Definition: Assignment. (1.) Meaningful*

*Meaningful* is an inside definition—no one else's opinion matters here. There is a connection between who you are inside, what you have experienced, and how being involved in this is meaningful to you. Very often there is some personal reason for taking this one on, which may have led to starting an organization or being part of it. For me, realizing what women's circles with a sacred center can do to support the life, the creativity, and the activism of its members, came from being in a prayer circle for decades (irreverently called "the Sisters of Perpetual Disorder") and the "mother circle of the Millionth Circle" for just over a decade.

Each year, when I attend presentations and panels given by women activists from NGOs at the

United Nations, I become aware of how many of them as young women were in need of the services that they provide, and are survivors who work to end abuses. Examples abound, such as the women who once were trafficked and now work to rescue trafficked women. Compassion in action called many activist women who were moved by the plight of young girls.

*Definition: Assignment (2.) Fun*

Fun—when you are with others who share your values, and with whom you can celebrate, laugh, mourn, or cry together at the ups and downs of the journey. When what you do matters and you feel and see that it makes a difference. When it uses your creativity and you find the courage to do it. When you can be so involved and absorbed in it that you lose track of time. You may never have worked so hard in your life, and yet never spent the time with more satisfaction.

However, every heart activist or creative woman in for the long run also knows that the definition of "fun" doesn't fit those times in which criticism rains down, when funds dry up, or worse, when people who you thought of as friends abandon, betray, or make fun of you. Or when you hear: "Who do you think you are?" During times that are clearly "not fun," if the assignment is a true one, it remains meaningful to you. Plus, there is truth in the saying, "activism is a cure for despair." Even in the worst of times, if you continue to be an activist and understand the principle of a tipping point—that when it is reached, it required all the actions and consciousness-raising that preceded it—you keep on keeping on.

*Definition: Assignment (3.) Motivated by Love*

*Motivated by love*—love for what you protect, or serve, or help—it could be a principle, people, animals, and nature. Love for beauty, for peace and harmony. To want for others what you are grateful to have. For many women who are becoming activists, spirituality came first. Love for the sacred feminine, for Gaia—the Earth as Great Mother, for Mother's Agenda: for all children to have what every mother wants for her own child.

Love is the only source of energy that is not zero-sum: if I give you anything else, you will have more and I'll have less. This is not so with love: the more love I give you, the more I have myself, the more you will have, and the more there will be in the world.

# MOVING TOWARD
# THE MILLIONTH CIRCLE

*Everyone who has been drawn to the idea of
"the millionth circle" is part of the millionth circle vision,
and any event or circle that anyone creates that
furthers the formation of more circles with a sacred center
can freely define what they are doing as being
part of the millionth circle movement*

—www.millionthcircle.org

# MOVING TOWARD
# THE MILLIONTH CIRCLE

A BOOK IS like a child to an author. When it goes out into the world, we do not know how it will be received, or how we will be changed through it. Also as every mother and involved father knows, worlds of people open up through one's child. When we think we are taking a child by the hand to meet people in the extended family, schools, or neighborhood, the child is taking us by the hand into relationships we would not have made on our own.

In 1999, I wrote a little book (the size of this one) that has had a big influence, and as a result, I inadvertently became the mother of a movement for a Fifth World Conference on Women (5WCW) at the United Nations. The little book was *The Millionth Circle: How to Change Ourselves and the World, the Essential Guide to Women's Circles.*

*The Millionth Circle* is a book, a metaphoric seed packet, and a metaphoric number. It inspires starting women's circles with a sacred center. It postulates that each new circle matters—and would contribute to an epic shift—because each contributes towards reaching the metaphoric *millionth circle* that would usher in a post-patriarchal era.

## *From Author to Advocate: First Steps*

Very soon after publication, the little book was taken by Peggy Sebera and Ronita Johnson to the Parliament of the World's Religions Conference in Cape Town, South Africa. They were co-leading a workshop, in which a documentary, *BeComing: Women's Circles, Women's Lives,* was the focus. Elly Pradervand from Geneva came to the workshop, as did Elinore Detiger from the Netherlands and Costa Rica. The book inspired them to envision forming an organization based on it. I first heard of this a few weeks later, when Peggy called me and told me about their idea and how they wanted my permission to use the name "millionth circle," and would I come to the first organizing meeting? Which, as it turned out, was to be held in Northern California, less than an hour's drive from my home. I said yes.

I could only attend the initial evening, and wasn't present for the discussions and decisions that led to The Millionth Circle Initiative. (*www. millionthcircle.org*). Of consequence to what has followed, among those who came were leaders from three United Nations NGOs: Pathways To Peace (Avon Mattison), Women's World Summit Foundation (Elly Pradervand), and Global Education Associates (Ann Smith). As a result of their presence and convictions and the intuitive rightness grasped by the others, there was from the beginning an intention to bring circles to the United Nations. This was how I came to events associated with the United Nations Commission on the Status of Women (CSW) in 2002 as a member of the "millionth circle"—the more formal-sounding name Millionth Circle Initiative has come to be known simply as "millionth circle." My book brought me to the UN.

*United Nations Initiation*

My first time at the UN was a consciousness-raising experience and the beginning of an education. In 2002, I went with others from the millionth circle for the Commission on the Status of Women meetings, where parallel events are presented and attended by women who help women and girls. Since then, I go every year. We in the United States rarely hear about the document agreed upon by nations to protect women and girls referred to by its initials CEDAW (Convention on the Elimination of All Forms of Discrimination Against Women) that has been signed by every country except the United States, Iran, and North Korea, (shame on us!); or about Security Council Resolution #1325, the Women, Peace and Security resolution, which if implemented would bring women into peace-making efforts before, during, and after conflicts.

Or that there are goals set by the UN and signed by its members to improve the status of women that many countries are working to meet, while others pay lip service to, or ignore—these major principles and goals are in the Beijing Platform for Action and the Millennium Development Goals.

Very little of what the UN does as a positive force for good reaches us through the mainstream media. Until I was there, I did not realize how significant the UN is to people in many parts of the world. A very imperfect institution, it nonetheless is like the beacon on the hill in the world of power and ongoing conflicts. Waiting in lines to register with women in colorful African garb, I learned that they were from neighboring countries, and could meet only in New York to compare notes and share ways that worked, and that many of them could come *only* because it was a UN event.

It was appalling to listen to panels and workshops given by non-governmental organizations that work to save girls and women from traffickers, give medical and reproductive health care, help women recover from rape, prevent female

genital mutilation, stop child marriages, edu-
cate, empower, provide resources, or work to
make human rights apply to women. Women are
treated like objects to be used, abused, raped, sold,
discarded, or murdered, for a variety of reasons.
Appalling things happen to women and girls when
we are treated as if we don't matter, are considered lesser beings, or as the possessions of men.
According to Amnesty International, one out of
three women worldwide—including those of us in
the industrialized world—will in our lifetime be
beaten, raped, or abused.

I was inspired as well as appalled. I listened to
the panel given by women from Sierra Leone who
participated in the peace negotiations that settled
their long civil war. It gave me food for thought
about how a critical number of women in decision-
making positions could change the world. I thought
it likely that only women in sufficient numbers and
influence could change the inevitability of conflict
and war.  In societies where male dominance and
male communication are about who is top dog, the
potential loss of status, property, or power triggers

deep-seated fears in men, leads to fight or flight/ adrenaline-testosterone reactions. The peace table then becomes one more arena to win or lose.

Women use conversation to understand and find similarities and solutions; under stress, this communication pattern leads to tend and befriend/oxytocin-estrogen reactions. In Sierra Leone, the Women, Peace and Security resolution or #1325 was imposed. As a result, these women were at the peace table as full partners. When neither side is humiliated and a balance of power is reached, peace between former enemies is potentially lasting. Growing up in patriarchy, women usually become experienced at helping men to save face and look good, and can be intuitive about where personal compromises can be made; men, on the other hand, grow up learning to assess power—amount held, who wields it and would use it. The differences in communication and physiology between men and women are complementary when this is so, which makes a negotiated peace agreement likely to succeed when both men and women mediate, negotiate, and work toward a settlement in which both sides do give up something and neither is left with a grudge or weapon supremacy.

I had mistakenly assumed when I first went to the UN in 2002 that there would be another women's conference in 2005. There had been four previous ones, the last in Beijing in 1995, and I expected the fifth one would happen in 2005. Forty thousand women attended in 1995; international women's leadership had been fostered by it; alliances and friendships resulted that made huge differences to individuals and that affected the leadership of organizations, countries, and the UN itself. I learned that there were no such plans for 2005, and was told that there would never be another one—the time for women's conferences was over. I came away disturbed by this news— to never have another UN women's conference felt intuitively wrong. Especially in the twenty-first century, with widespread use of the Internet, social networking, new technologies, and the potential of bringing circles with a sacred center to an intergenerational global women's conference.

The "millionth circle" was a metaphoric number inspired by the story of the "Hundredth Monkey," which had inspired the anti-nuclear proliferation activists to keep on keeping on when conventional wisdom said it was foolish to think that ordinary citizens could stop the nuclear arms race which was part of the "Cold War" between the (now former) Soviet Union (USSR) and the United States. If by accident or on purpose a nuclear warhead was sent by one of them toward the other, there would be instant, massive retaliation. Grassroots activism, dissemination of scientific information such as how "nuclear winter" would descend on the planet, and a reduction in the demonization of Russia through citizen diplomacy and other means helped prepare the way for conversations between the American president, Ronald Reagan, and Russian premier, Michail Gorbachev, and their signing of the Non-Nuclear Proliferation treaty. Grassroots activism works from the bottom up to influence leaders at the top.

The hundredth monkey was an allegory based on the premise of theoretical biologist Rupert

Sheldrake's "morphic field theory," which postulates that the behavior of a species changes when a critical number of them learn to do a new thing. The morphic field for humans is the collective unconscious described by C.G. Jung, only this emphasis is more on the collective than the individual. When something new is adopted by a critical mass of people, a new idea or behavior, one that may even be greatly resisted, then becomes a new norm. The same point is reached through geometric progression, as described by Malcolm Gladwell in *The Tipping Point*. Such was the case for getting American women the right to vote, which took from 1848 to 1920, as well as an explanation for the accomplishments of the Women's Movement, from the end of the 1960s through the 1970s. Consciousness-raising groups in the United States brought ideas such as stereotyping, sexism, feminism, and patriarchy into the culture, which led to changes in laws and attitudes in less than a decade.

Circles spread in the same way that strawberry plants grow more of themselves. They send out runners; each one that finds fertile ground will start a new strawberry plant, and each new plant in turn will then send out runners to take root, until the field is full of strawberry plants. Women who are in circles who tell others about them, encourage more circles to form; when the idea takes root a new circle forms. Simple how this works. Morphic field research supports the idea that the more circles there are, the faster and easier others will form, each new one then contributes toward reaching the metaphoric millionth circle, and all are contributing to making it easier and faster for others to form.

My little book had brought me to the UN, knowing what I did about what a proliferation of circles could do for the women in them, and how organically they can grow in numbers. When I learned that there would not be another UN women's conference, it struck me as a huge loss of an opportunity to accelerate change towards equality and empowerment of women, through which we would end patriarchy for the good of all. In becoming an advocate for 5WCW, the same principle of critical mass, bottom-up activism would hold. In fact, there is a synergy between seeding circles and advocating for a global women's conference.

The proliferation of women's circles—which form easier and faster, the more there are—would result in a world fit for all children and therefore for all on the planet. When there are a critical number of empowered, aware women, then what can result is what every woman wants for her own children and what all children are entitled to have. This is mothers' agenda: clean air to breathe, safe water to drink, nourishing food, universal education and access to excellent health care, where all have opportunities to develop intellectually, emotionally, and spiritually, where there is compassion and justice, and *no one* lives in fear of abuse or violence or war.

# 4

THE STONE CUTTERS

*Hope is an orientation of spirit, hope is an orientation of the heart. It is not the certainty that something will turn out well, but the conviction that something makes sense no matter how it turns out.*

—Vaclev Havel

# THE STONE CUTTERS

Three stone cutters were working in a marble quarry.

Each was hard at work, shaping a large stone into a block.

A visitor came and watched them.

○

The visitor asked the first stone cutter, "What are you doing?"

His reply, "Isn't it obvious? I'm making a block."

○

He asked the second stone cutter, "What are you doing?"

His reply, "I'm making this for a wall."

○

Then he asked the third stone cutter, "What are you doing?"

His reply, "I'm helping build a cathedral that will last a thousand years."

○

It wouldn't be hard to guess, everything else being equal, that the third stone cutter had the greatest job satisfaction, because his work had meaning beyond the immediate task. It would also be likely that he would take more care and pride in the work he was doing because he was participating in a significant undertaking.

One major source of meaning we have comes from connecting with or becoming part of something bigger than ourselves: a project that helps others, a chance to make the world a better place. In *Reality is Broken*, Jane McGonigal writes: "Meaning is something we're all looking for more of:

more ways to make a difference in the bigger picture, more chances to leave a lasting mark on the world, more moments of awe and wonder at the scale of projects and communities we are part of." In summing up her findings, she concluded that the single best way to add meaning to our lives is "to connect our daily actions to something bigger than ourselves—and the bigger the better."

The idea of contributing toward the millionth circle and a global women's conference to accelerate this fits being part of something bigger, but like the stone cutters, what you are doing beyond that which is obvious to see has to be held in your mind. If you form a new circle or meet regularly in an ongoing circle with a sacred center, each time the circle comes together, it contributes to the morphic field for your particular circle and to the archetype of the circle in the collective unconscious. This would be true whether you are aware of it or not. However, when there is a conscious intention to add to this circle toward the metaphoric millionth circle, and the intention is invoked, something subtly shifts. The familiar circle takes on a deeper significance: we feel that we are participating in in a shared bond and furthering a vision. This is an intuitive or felt link.

I believe that conscious intentions are *thoughts bonded to energy*. The thought comes to mind, is put into words. Then it is *taken to heart*—which is more than an expression. We can also hold and mold intentions, incubating and growing them. Our intentions go ahead of us into time, and at some point can manifest through new accomplishments, shifts, or materialization of the intention. We become part of a movement when great numbers of people hold the same intention or vision as we do.

I feel momentum is growing toward the millionth circle from observing how women influence discussions and the decision process when they are in a position to do so. Conversational collaboration comes easily when women are involved as equals with men in the workplace and in organizations as well as in egalitarian personal relationships. The simple act of asking for a pause in the midst of a heated discussion (reflection, centering, moment of stillness, inner check in) invites in the morphic field/archetype of the circle with a sacred center. Moreover, when the idea of the millionth circle is shared, a level of meaning is added that some will grasp and take to heart.

# 5

# SOVEREIGNTY

*I will choose what enters me,*
*what becomes flesh of my flesh.*
*Without choice, no politics, no ethics lives.*
*My life is a non-negotiable demand.*

—Marge Piercy, "Right to Life"

# SOVEREIGNTY

## *King Arthur's Quest:*
## *What Do Women Want?*

There is a story about King Arthur

who had a year to answer the question,

"What do women want?"

○

His life was on the line

spared if he can answer the question,

forfeit it, if not.

○

Then Gawain

the most chivalrous and handsome knight

in his kingdom

took the challenge.

To find an answer or pay the price.

○

Dame Ragnell,

The most ugly old hag, the loathly damsel

knew the answer to the question.

That which women want more than anything

is "sovereignty"

○

Her price for this answer

was marriage to Gawain.

○

On the wedding night, Gawin could hardly bear to look at his bride.

kissed her with his eyes closed,

a kiss that transformed her into the most beautiful woman

he had ever seen.

As dawn approached,

Dame Ragnell said, "You must choose.

Either I will be beautiful by day when the world can see me,

Or ugly by day and beautiful at night for you alone."

What do you suppose he chose?

○

Gawain said, "Be beautiful when you want to be"

Which meant she would have sovereignty over herself.

○

"Sovereignty" is a word that if used at all, generally refers to a sovereign nation. It means *autonomy, independence, liberty, self-determination, self-governance, and freedom.*

Personal sovereignty has a similar meaning to a woman. Does her body belong to her? Does she have the same legal rights as a man, the same access to education and work as her brother? Can she own property in her own name, keep her own wages? Can she decide whether to marry or not, and to whom? Is she free to choose if and where she worships? Do human rights apply to her?

The opposite of sovereignty is submission.

## Declaration of Independence

The desire for sovereignty motivated the thirteen American colonies to revolt against the British Empire which ruled over them, taxed them, conscripted their homes to house troops, made them a vassal-state to be exploited. Grievances and rights, including the right to revolt, were stated in The Declaration of Independence, July 4, 1776, with the ringing statement: "We hold these truths to be self-evident, that all men are created equal, that they are endowed by their Creator with certain unalienable Rights, that among these are life, liberty, and the pursuit of happiness."

## *Declaration of Sentiments*

In 1848, The Declaration of Sentiments was adopted at the first women's rights convention held in Seneca Falls, New York. It contained the exact inalienable Rights statement with a significant addition: "We hold these truths to be self-evident: that *all men and women* are created equal . . ." The list of grievances were those in which men held absolute tyranny over women. The first was that women were not permitted to vote—did not have suffrage. Efforts to gain this right would take from 1848 until 1920. In 1848, a woman was legally compelled to obey her husband. He had legal rights over all property, even over the wages she earned. Domestic abuse was legal; he could physically punish her with a stick (as long as it was not thicker than his thumb in one law).

## Universal Declaration of Human Rights

In December 1948, the UN General Assembly adopted the Universal Declaration of Human Rights, Palais de Chaillot, Paris. This arose directly out of the experience of World War II, and was the first global statement on the rights to which all human beings are entitled. It was followed by a series of Covenants, which were signed by a sufficient number of countries, that together comprise the International Bill of Rights with the force of international law in 1976.

## Earth Charter

Earth Charter: the idea originated in 1987 with the final text adopted in March 2000 at UNESCO headquarters in Paris. Preamble: *We stand at a critical moment in Earth's history, a time when humanity must choose its future. As the world becomes increasingly interdependent and fragile, the future at once holds great peril and great promise. To move forward we must recognize that in the midst of a magnificent diversity of cultures and life forms we are one human family and one Earth community with a common destiny. We must join together to bring forth a sustainable global society founded on respect for nature, universal human rights, economic justice, and a culture of peace. Towards this end, it is imperative that we, the peoples of Earth, declare our responsibility to one another, to the greater community of life, and to future generations.*

## *Beijing Platform for Action*

In Beijing, China in 1994, forty thousand attended the Fourth UN World Conference on Women (4WCW), where the theme voiced by Hillary Clinton became: "Human Rights are Women's Rights, Women's Rights are Human Rights." The Beijing Platform for Action listed twelve areas of concern in which progress is needed for women to gain equal rights and human rights:

- The persistent and increasing burden of poverty on women
- Inequalities and inadequacies in and unequal access to education and training

- Inequalities and inadequacies in and unequal access to health care and related services

- Violence against women

- The effects of armed or other kinds of conflict on women, including those living under foreign occupation

- Inequality in economic structures and policies, in all forms of productive activities and in access to resources

- Inequality between men and women in the sharing of power and decision-making at all levels

- Insufficient mechanisms at all levels to promote the advancement of women

- Lack of respect for and inadequate promotion and protection of the human rights of women

- Stereotyping of women and inequality in women's access to and participation in all communication systems, especially in the media

- Gender inequalities in the management of natural resources and in the safe-guarding of the environment
- Persistent discrimination against and violation of the rights of the girl

## *The Opposite of Sovereignty is Submission*

Speaking truth to power

Is a challenge in intimate relationships.

Not just in the world.

Transforming a hierarchy into circle when such is the case

means becoming a heart-centered activist.

a transformer of your private piece of the patriarchy

into an egalitarian one.

It will have a ripple effect

in your family

through generations even.

O

Heart-centered activists need support from others

whether at the home front or in the trenches for social justice.

It matters when trustworthy others know what you are doing

are aware of your vulnerability and courage,

of the risks you may be taking.

Women who will watch your back,

will pray for you, will stay in touch,

speak from their own experience,

and keep in confidence what was said in confidence.

O

In other words, every heart-centered activist

needs to be in a circle with a sacred center.

# 6

## CIRCLE OR/AND HIERARCHY

*I am only one, but still I am one.*
*I cannot do everything,*
*but still I can do something.*
*I will not refuse to do the something I can do.*

—Helen Keller

# CIRCLE OR/AND HIERARCHY

Every Relationship of Two

is Either a Circle or a Hierarchy

O

It's a circle when love is at the center

of a voluntarily entered relationship,

And the feelings, priorities, and values of each person

matter to the other.

When confidences are kept and are not fodder for gossip

And vulnerabilities are not exploited.

It's a circle when truth can be told

however painful to say

About oneself

Or to the other.

O

In any circle relationship

There will be bumps on the road

Misunderstandings, misperceptions, or just plain thoughtlessness

come up between ourselves

and friends,

spouses or partners of any kind.

O

When unspoken mistrust or resentment arises

And only one of the two knows when it got there,

then it is that person's responsibility

to speak of it.

Might it be possible to be curious and not judgmental

to check out what was going on and why

when something is hurtful.

○

Your truth is how it made you feel.

Everything else is speculation.

A circle of two can become a growth medium.

Where a field of trust can deepen

if the truth of how one truly feels or fears

can be voiced.

It helps to own one's own vulnerability

otherwise it is hidden under anger and judgment

which easily provokes defensiveness

and more anger in return.

Not a pretty picture and not what each truly wants

in a  circle relationship.

O

In a hierarchy-patriarchy of two,

the agreement, stated or not:

One of the two is more important than the other.

One of the two can freely express feelings, needs, priorities,

and prejudices,

or make demands on the other.

With no expectations of reciprocity.

O

In a hierarchy-patriarchy of two

One is more important and entitled than the other,

is in control.

A pattern that leads one to become the narcissist,

and the other to be co-dependent.

This is the form of patriarchal marriage,

which is not between equals.

○

Adult children of alcoholics had to practice co-dependency,

learned to stuff their own feelings.

Unreasonable, emotionally out of control people

have this effect on others also.

○

"Speaking Truth to Power,"

is called for in any relationship of two that is a hierarchy.

It is the person in the role of co-dependent

who by finding her voice and courage

to speak up,

begins a dialogue with the other

makes it possible to transform a patriarchal relationship

into a circle or leave it.

○

Remember Eleanor Roosevelt's words:

"No one can make you feel inferior without your consent."

○

## *Circle and Hierarchy: Tension of Opposites*

In Jungian theory and practice, one particular concept—*the tension of opposites*—comes to mind often. Within us, as between us and others, there can be an either-or choice of what to do, or how to do it. In the psyche, this tension may arise between heart and mind, between competing priorities, or loyalties. When this comes up, effort is made to become conscious of what is operating within us, and to stay with the tension until there is clarity: once choice becomes clear. Or we hold both until a new resolution comes, that is not either-or. Jung called it the transcendent function. The new resolution is a creative third, something that arises out of the tension that is better than either choice.

Circle and hierarchy are in creative tension in successful teams, functioning families, and in democracies. In a circle, everyone matters, leadership is shared, and consensus is sought. In a functioning family, everyone matters and there is a hierarchy; parents are responsible for their children, consensus may be sought on some matters, and as children grow older, they are expected to take on more responsibilities and make more choices for themselves. In functioning families, there is a meld of circle and hierarchy based on experience, age, and responsibility. *Love is at the center.* In dysfunctional families, someone rules the roost and exercises power over others through the threat of emotional or physical abuse, which puts fear rather than love at the center. The most blatant hierarchy is a dictatorship.

### People with Sovereignty

The premise of a democracy is that everyone matters and that there are checks and balances on power, including the power of the ballot. Ideally there are just laws that are applied equally and fairly. This is the premise of the Bill of Rights and the Constitution—which initially applied only to white men, was extended to black men, and then to women. The thirteen original colonies and subsequent new states retained areas of sovereignty when they chose to become one of the United States of America. Every four years, the fact that it takes a majority of Electoral College votes, and not a majority of votes cast, to elect a president is a reminder of the retention of sovereignty by the states. Circle vs. hierarchy is reflected in the two-party system: if each had a ballot symbol, the Democratic Party's could be a circle for its everybody matters inclusiveness, and the hierarchical values of the Republicans could be represented by a triangle. When the two parties are able to collaborate and compromise, legislation is the result of a tension of opposites.

Successful teams are made up of people who voluntarily subordinate their individual wills to accomplish something together that could not be done by one person alone. One person may be the captain of the team, another might be the visible star or high scorer, but there is among themselves a recognition of each other's contribution to the team effort. When each is at the top of his or her game, using talent that took dedication and years to develop, there is a beauty of form and achievement. They are also having fun. While this sounds like a sports metaphor and I did have in mind watching the Olympics and the American women's soccer team in particular, I also think of surgical teams that work together with a fluidity of motion, each anticipating what is needed next, almost as of one mind. Here there is a hierarchy—the chief surgeon is in charge, except when it is the anesthesiologist, which it can be in some emergencies. All are positioned around the patient on the operating table, whose life or quality of life depends upon what they do together. When the surgery is done and the incision sutured, all share in the mutual accomplishment. Amateurs who perform a play or a concert after hours and hours of rehearsal have similar feelings when the curtain goes down and they are applauded, as do amateur teams who know when they play well. Someone directs, conducts, or calls the plays—there is some hierarchy and it is also a circle. Like sovereign states, these are voluntary efforts made by people who freely affiliate.

### *I-Thou or I-It*

This is a simple distinction between circle and hierarchy: whether people treat others as a "thou" or as an "it." All of the great documents and declarations in Western history define inherent rights to dignity, respect, justice. I think of them as being steps in the direction of defining other people, as well as all living things, and the planet itself as having sacred rights: which is to be a *thou* rather than an *it*. Where there is love, I-Thou is also. Documents such as those already mentioned, and the Magna Carta, were directed toward men in power who ruled over others—by divine right, then political right.

*Lessons from Wild Geese*

It was fun for me to compare wild geese flying in "V" formation to women's circles in *Urgent Message from Mother*. Except for the shape, a circle functions as geese do. They rotate leadership—when the lead goose tires, another takes the lead position. By flying in formation, they fly 71 percent further together than one goose could fly alone. As each goose flaps its wings it creates an uplift that supports the goose flying behind it. The support of the others makes it easier to go where they want to go. They honk while in flight to encourage the lead goose to keep up the speed. The lessons are applicable—we do go further with support of others; their thoughts, ideas, and prayers add an uplift, and our "honking" does need to be encouraging. I've ended some workshop circles where I talked about

Lessons from Wild Geese in a lighthearted, playful way—I had participants be pretend geese, flapping arms as wings and honking. It's also been a delight when, from time to time, I get an email that ends with "Honk! Honk! Honk!"

# 7

PATH WITH HEART

*Listen, listen, listen to my heart song.*
*Listen, listen, listen to my heart song.*
*I will never forget you*
*I will never forsake you*
*I will never forget you*
*I will never forsake you*
*Listen, listen, listen to my heart song.*
*Listen, listen, listen to my heart song.*

—Paramhansa Yogananda

# PATH WITH HEART

I imagined being in the high desert of northern Mexico

with Carlos Castaneda

then a graduate student at UCLA

listening to Don Juan,

the indigenous shaman, teacher, mentor, and most likely

an intended dissertation subject at the time.

It is in the middle of nowhere.

There are mesquite bushes and little else to be seen.

Small trails made by animals,

traces of rivulets,

signs of a passing thunderstorm that made little impact.

○

Don Juan says that anything is one of a million paths,

all paths are the same.

None of them go anywhere.

Like those we see going through the bush or into the bush.

And yet, we must carefully and consciously choose a path,

we must ask ourselves,

"Does this path have heart?"

○

There is a good reason to ask.

There is truth to what Don Juan had to say:

Traveling on a path with heart makes for a joyful journey,

"as long as you follow it, you are one with it."

But if you chose a path out of fear or ambition,

you will come to curse your life.

One makes you strong, the other weakens you.

○

One must learn to follow

the inner beat of intuitive feeling

to be on a path with heart.

to trust your heart chakra

that receptive place in the center of your chest

that aches in sorrow and loss

feels the pain of others

and bubbles through you in joy.

It is a personal compass.

That discerns what direction to take.

○

"Does this path have heart?"

is more than a warm, fuzzy feeling.

○

It can be powerful, immediate recognition,

A call (as in vocation) and a response (yes!)

○

"Does this path have heart?"

takes you to a crossroad, a potential fork in the path.

Becomes a time for reflection,

to take stock

who are you and what you are doing

with "your one wild and precious life."

(a phrase from a Mary Oliver poem).

Pay attention that time is passing,

while you dither.

"Doesn't everything die at last, and too soon?"

○

To be a heart-centered activist

Or an advocate on behalf of justice and compassion

to help women and girls, mothers and children

animals, trees, disabled people, the disempowered, and ignored

is called forth by circumstance

by the inner voice that says, "silence is consent."

Or by the knowledge that to do nothing is a choice.

And the inner questions,

Are you part of the problem (apathy)

or part of the solution (activist)?

O

A time for Action

O

There is at this time in history,

yet another motivation to be a heart-centered activist,

this is the call to enlist strong women

to empower women to become strong

to partner with men in making decisions

that matter to families and to the world.

Energizing a global women's movement

O

To infuse women's wisdom into patriarchal cultures

until culture changes.

# 8

## THE DALAI LAMA
## AND THE MILLIONTH CIRCLE

*No matter what is happening*
*No matter what is going on around you*
*Never Give Up.*

—H.H. the XIV Dalai Lama

# THE DALAI LAMA
# AND THE MILLIONTH CIRCLE

WHEN I THINK of the Dalai Lama, I smile to myself, and I feel a warm spot in my heart for him. I remember when I first met him in 1986, as part of a small private audience in the Netherlands, which I wrote about in *Crossing to Avalon*. This journey marked the beginning of a mid-life pilgrimage to sacred sites, and in retrospect, an awakening of my heart-chakra as a perceptive organ that responds to sacred sites and to people who carry in themselves a connection to the sacred feminine. These are men and women who are following a path with heart that is meaningful, fun, and motivated by love in the midst of the reality of the world. When I met His Holiness, who exemplifies this, I was charmed by the unexpected chortling happy sounds he made in between answering questions. I sensed a deep and wide energy field about him (wished I could see auras and not just feel them!). He was an unexpected combination of a wise person and a joyful child, which is a particularly sustaining combination of qualities in activists. The healing laughter of being in the same boat together—as in a circle with a sacred center—keeps us centered and able to draw from Source.

Since this first meeting, I have been with the Dalai Lama seven more times—three on stage together at conferences, usually preceded by small gatherings with him beforehand. His influence is in this book in ways that I want to share. Meetings with him and quotes from him lead me to muse or ponder upon the meaning of his presence and his words. In C.G. Jung's psychological vocabulary, which bridges spirituality, mythology, and the psyche, the Dalai Lama constellates the archetype of meaning which Jung called the Self. When ego (our sense of "I") aligns itself with the archetype of meaning, synchronicities happen—meaningful coincidences that cannot be explained by logic or cause and effect. This is our experience of the invisible world taking an interest in us. It's what people speak of as angels, archetypes, and ancestors, or the universe gently intervening. Synchronicities are recognized by the heart with the mind as observer; heart feels grace and gratitude, and often when it is a *big* synchronicity, a sense of wonder.

At the *Conference on the Search for the True Meaning of Peace,* held in Costa Rica in June 1989, I introduced my daughter Melody and son Andy backstage to His Holiness and to Thomas Berry, Catholic priest and eco-theologian, whose vision was that we humans are part of a cosmological story, sharing our story with the Earth and the Cosmos. I wanted my children to meet them then, and I mention Thomas Berry here, because of the bigness of his heart and vision—in him, I saw another wise elder with a glowing inner child. This conference was under the auspices of the UN University for Peace, and was an early connection with people who were working toward a culture of peace. Costa Rica was a peaceful country without a standing army; its president, Oscar Arias, was a Nobel Peace Prize laureate. As it is situated in the narrow isthmus of Central America between Nicaragua and Panama, there were marked differences between Costa Rica and its unstable neighbors. In Nicaragua, armed conflict between the Sandinistas and Contras had wrecked the economy and demoralized the people, many of whom had fled the country. Panama was under the military dictatorship and oppressive rule of Manuel Noriega. In contrast, Costa Rica had the benefits of peace—a stable society and prosperity. Environmentally responsible efforts successfully created and preserved national rain forests and fostered ecotourism. It was my first opportunity to visit a cloud rain forest in the mountains. What a difference peace makes, not just to the people but to sustaining nature and beauty.

## Compassionate Action and Freedom

In October 1989, this time in Newport Beach, California, I was one of seven psychiatrists and psychologists who were in three days of onstage dialogue with the Dalai Lama. These conversations were transcribed and edited in *Worlds in Harmony*. This conference developed from His Holiness's wish to learn about the relationship between Buddhist and Western psychology. A few days later, we learned that he would be awarded the Nobel Peace Prize. I came away needing to think more about the conversation on *compassionate action*. I was challenged by the Dalai Lama's conviction that action accompanies real compassion. He maintained that it is not enough to feel for people and their pain or troubles. Empathy or sympathy is not enough to qualify as compassion.

If compassion and action must go together as he said, I wondered about what I do in my office. What is it that talk-therapists and analysts do? I see that these sessions help people. How to make sense of his statement in this context? He made me think, and as a result, I stretched the usual meaning of action. I thought first about the activist and advocacy I know about through *doing*: speaking up for a principle, the meetings, positions taken, picketing (once), writing this book. Then I thought about what *I am doing* when I listen to what people tell me of their lives. As a Jungian analyst and psychiatrist, the listening is active and empathic. I function as a witness to people's lives and help them to see the patterns and meaning in what they tell me, and respond differently than expected with understanding instead of judgment. These are quiet acts of *doing*. Often, the inner work is about remembering and reconnecting, and the outer work is about supporting them to find ways to satisfy needs for growth, intimacy, creativity, spirituality, integrity—which is to become our own advocate on behalf of who we are or were meant to be.

When women who are the empathic gender support the reality of the past and aspirations for the future of each other, listening with compassion is doing something to support these same potentials. This is what circles with a sacred center can do for the women in them, drawing upon their collective experience and collective wisdom, and the energy of the archetype of meaning.

The answer to the question, "What do women want?" that King Arthur needed to save his life, and

Freud is famously known for not knowing, was "sovereignty." I recall an image from the onstage dialogue with the Dalai Lama. He pointed his index finger vigorously at the large vein visible at his wrist, and said: "Freedom! Freedom! It is in the blood." A vivid way of saying that freedom or sovereignty is an instinct—something innate that we all desire. Efforts to overthrow dictators, toss out occupying forces, and resist colonialization would come from this fundamental desire.

It is what drives the Tibetans in Tibet to resist China's efforts to subdue their spirit and spirituality and the recognition of others to support the Tibetans in exile in Dharamsala, India. How to gain sovereignty without taking on the characteristics of the oppressor motivates non-violent resistance. This was the path of Mahatma Gandhi and Martin Luther King, Jr. It is also the path taken by millions or billions of unknown women, who are and have been oppressed in their homes by their husbands with the support of religion and custom. Yet they are often on a path with heart due to their maternal love of children, the laughter and delight that women can share together, and the ability to forgive the oppressive husband, many of whom mellow as they grow older. The Dalai Lama's way of resisting China's use of power and neither becoming numb or urging retaliation is, when I think of it, a path with heart; that is also women's way. The two elements in him, a wise elder and spontaneous child (that part in adults who can feel with and for others, cry, giggle, laugh, and be playful), are present in women of all ages once they are past being self-conscious, when heart remains engaged in life. In patriarchy, this spontaneous inner child is usually bullied out of boys and men.

## Midlife and Older Women
### Becoming Activists

San Francisco was the site of the next conference with the Dalai Lama—his presence is the recollection that made it memorable for me, and why I accepted the invitation to participate in the first place. All the presenters were onstage for this last plenary of the conference. As is so for so many conferences, the audience had a preponderance of women of midlife and older—who were listening to men speaking about passing the torch to the younger generation, and young men speaking about their responsibility to take it on.

It prodded an "enough of this" feeling in me which led me to speak with some passion about the baby boomer generation of women that was so well-represented in the audience. In numbers, education, travel, responsibilities, resources, networks—there has never been a generation like this in history, who *could* change the world. It is not just the younger generation that needs to step up to the plate right now, I said, but the boomer generation who were the immediate beneficiaries of the women's movement. After fifty and in good health, a woman can have decades of active life ahead of her. Feminism gave us a sense of sisterhood, life provides lessons in loss and in gratitude, time provides perspective. This conviction that women who came into adulthood after the women's movement in the 1970s are an enormous untapped resource for social justice and peaceful resolutions has continued to grow. It led to writing *Crones Don't Whine* and *Goddesses in Older Women* to empower the generation of women over fifty. This was followed by *Urgent Message from Mother,* in which I specifically urged, "Gather the Women, Save the World."

## Synchronicity

The next connection with the Dalai Lama was in 2007 at a conference in Munich. This conference was under his auspices. He had been stricken and been quite sick when he had been in India, many months before. This was his first public experience since then. It was a very important theoretical conference to introduce *Tendral,* an ancient Tibetan Buddhist teaching that is compatible with contemporary Western thinking. It brought together quantum physicists, philosophers, immunologists, psychologists. My subject was synchronicity—a phenomenon observed by C.G. Jung, and a word coined by him to name meaningful coincidences that are impossible to explain by cause and effect.

In my first book, *The Tao of Psychology: Synchronicity and the Self,* I saw how synchronicity in western psychology could be equated with the underlying oneness or Tao of Eastern philosophy. If I am involved in something that has meaning for me, synchronicities happen: they provide feedback, commentary, help in the form of the people who come into my life then, stories that inspire or fit what I am doing. Each time I get synchronistic help, which is often, it feels like grace, as if the universe is supporting what I am doing. It is invisible support that awes and humbles me even though it is not uncommon; to take notice of such things is somewhat like paying attention to dreams. I think that synchronicities are happening all the time to people and that like dreams, they are outer events that connect with the archetypal layer of our psyches and often speak to us in metaphors.

In the meeting beforehand, His Holiness looked well, and when asked what the effect of his illness had been on him, his comment was it deepened his experience of suffering and compassion. Twenty-plus years had gone by since we first met, and in the photo with the speakers, he is holding my hand in the front row. The wise elder was there, and the twinkle in his eye and hand in mine, attested to the ongoing presence of the archetype I'll now call the divine child—which is an archetype in us all—seen initially in the newborn, kept or lost along the way to adulthood and old age.

## Will We Live Up to This Prediction?

At the Vancouver Peace Summit for Nobel Laureates (2009), the Dalai Lama said, "The world will be saved by the western woman." Or as some of the tweets that went viral online had it, "The world will be saved by western women." While it has been a call to activism for some American and Canadian women, it had me pondering—if this were so, how would it come about? And why the western woman or western women, when the green uprising and Arab Spring, the International Women's Day demonstrations and marches are held elsewhere in the world, and the Convention Eliminating Discrimination Against Women (CEDAW) can't even get passed through the United States congress?

The Dalai Lama's phrase is provocative and encouraging. I have sat with the question: how might we save the world? The answer I came up with: it could become true if western women join a global women's movement in the twenty-first century to empower women worldwide that leads to an egalitarian world in which decisions that affect children, environment, peace, economy, the health and well-being of all uses both feminine and masculine principles. If we—the privileged women of the world—are the missing ingredient that makes this possible, then we must become heart-activists. To stay this course is best done with the support of circles with a sacred center. And, by doing so, we will also contribute our circles toward the metaphoric millionth circle and the end of patriarchy.

## The Western Woman

Is privileged

Lives longer, educated, has resources,

can choose to stay or move on

at stages of her life.

Values independence over obedience

as a principle.

○

Contributes to changing the world

as a wife and mother

by her example

raising sons and daughters

to be whole people,

whole-brained and whole-hearted.

○

Works at whatever she does

Grows through having responsibilities,

Can speak her mind

and take compassionate action.

○

The western woman

got herself the right to vote.

○

The suffragists in Seneca Falls

met around a round table

and wrote the Declaration of Sentiments

and organized the first women's rights convention.

Some picketed the White House,

were called unpatriotic, loose women,

were arrested and ridiculed.

And in time,

prevailed.

It may be annoying

but a movement is successful

when gains made are taken for granted.

O

Haven't we always had the right to vote?

O

Events moved much faster in the second half of the 1960s

Consciousness-raising groups caught on,

and "just women talking" became the Women's Movement

of the 1970s.

Equal pay for equal work,

equal access to education and equal opportunities.

Sisterhood and egalitarian marriage.

The personal is political.

"Ms."

became a declaration of personal sovereignty.

And Roe v. Wade

gave women reproductive rights,

sovereignty over her own body.

This was the second wave of feminism.

○

Right now,

The patriarchy is trying to set the clock back,

taking aim at reproductive rights

alpha males, religious fundamentalists

want women to be obedient

to know their place as inferiors.

○

Can't put the genie back in the bottle

women's spirit of sovereignty,

autonomy, independence

is contagious and freed.

○

Circles with a sacred center

support the women in them to become empowered,

to believe in themselves, to act upon their perceptions,

to make changes in their world.

Each circle and each time a circle meets

adds to the millionth circle morphic field.

makes it easier for more to form,

moving us toward a critical mass,

tipping point.

The metaphoric millionth circle.

○

A UN Global Conference on Women

would bring a hundred thousand influential women together

backed by supportive men,

millions more via Internet connections,

Heart-centered activists

supporting, equality, and empowerment,

women's rights as human rights,

adding more circles with a sacred center

to those already formed.

○

Women's wisdom, the sacred feminine,

compassionate action

are related to the feminine principle

of affiliation, receptivity, intuition, empathy, and interrelatedness.

Leads to fulfilling Mother's Agenda

for all children to have what we want for our own.

Leads to peace.

○

Think also of another global circle movement

of circles with a sacred center,

men and women

who call upon spiritual resources by whatever name,

share the truth of their lives

help each other, by helping themselves.

Keep in confidence what was said in confidence.

This is Alcoholics Anonymous,

and all the recovery groups based on AA

○

A suggestion.

If you are a "friend of Bill W."

speak at a meeting

ask that this circle add its energy

to the metaphoric millionth circle.

○

Under patriarchy

it is not just women who are oppressed.

The feminine principle is also

○

There is a boys-into-men program

learned in the home and schoolyard.

The rules and regulations are

enforced by humiliation and bullying:

Bury feelings, hide vulnerability and dependency

Don't be a baby, don't be a girl, don't be a sissy.

Don't talk about feelings,

Better yet, don't have any feelings

except anger.

The macho-model

which can be lonely, empty, and sad.

Numbing helps when this is painful.

Which is the why of most addictions.

○

The feminine potential in every man

begins with the dreamy, intuitive, touchy-feely emotional

little boy who came as an innocent into the world,

relates to the right half of the human brain,

that is poetic, metaphoric, imaginative,

and will atrophy over time

when unused.

○

1970s bumper sticker:

"The woman that needs liberating is the woman in every man."

Still true, but not for men

with post-women's movement mothers,

and fathers who were in the delivery room

and grew up in egalitarian families.

○

The left-brain is intellectual, logical

is naturally hierarchal, rational, favors either/or positions.

Something is either right or wrong, good or bad, superior or inferior.

Anything that can be measured or scientifically proven

is the stuff on which the left brain thrives.

○

The Western woman has the benefit of education.

left-brain development follows.

She can enter any profession or occupation

(thanks to the women's movement)

And as a woman who multi-tasks, raises children,

thinks about what to make for dinner,

is in a world of relationships,

and the arts as well,

Develops both sides of her symmetrical brain.

○

If it is up to women,

especially the Western woman

to save the world,

we would be wise to draw from

the wisdom of the original Western woman,

Indigenous Native American women

embodied in the Council of Grandmothers,

the wise women elders

of the Seneca Nations,

also known as the Iroquois Confederacy,

from which the framers of the American Constitution

drew their inspiration for checks and balances

and governance

with two exceptions.

They did not adopt

a principle of equality between men and women

and the council of wisewomen.

○

This council of elected grandmothers

decided the priorities

for the people,

met in council—which is circle—and made decisions by consensus,

even about going to war.

Every decision

takes into consideration

seven previous generations,

(a way to learn from history so as not to repeat it),

and considered potential consequences

on seven generations to come.

Beyond child-bearing themselves,

their own children now adults,

Their concern was for the well-being of all the children

of all of the tribes of the Seneca Nations.

◯

The Dalai Lama said

The Western woman will save the world.

Think history

How might this come about?

◯

One age is followed by another.

As the old gives way

Beliefs shift, power moves.

Initial turmoil at the threshold.

◯

Now is such a time.

Geopolitics, climate change, epidemics

The Internet, instant news, technology

The idea of democracy

A predicted cosmological change

comes into consciousness.

○

It is the Western Woman

who has the resources including connections

to bring the women of the world together

at a global conference on women.

energizing a worldwide women's movement

for empowerment and equality

of women, the feminine principle, and the sacred feminine.

Moving us toward the metaphoric millionth circle

To a post-patriarchal era

that saved the world.

# APPRECIATION

The Conveners of the Millionth Circle Initiative, Sisters of Perpetual Disorder (my prayer circle), Carol Hansen Grey for the *5wcw.org* website.

The 5WCW Circle of Advisors, and the many thousands of individuals who signed the online petition. Core circle support: Avon Mattison, Anele Heiges, Elly Pradervand, Marilyn Fowler, Anwarul K. Chowdhury, Donna Goodman, Rosemary Williams, Patricia Smith Melton, Jackie Weatherspoon. Jan Johnson, editor and publisher of Conari Press.

## About the Author

Jean Shinoda Bolen, M.D. is a Jungian analyst, psychiatrist, author and activist, a Distinguished Life Fellow of the American Psychiatric Association and former clinical professor of psychiatry at UCSF. She is an internationally known speaker and the author of twelve influential books in over eighty foreign translations, beginning with *The Tao of Psychology, Goddesses in Everywoman,* and *Gods in Everyman;* her last four books, including *Urgent Message from Mother: Gather the Women, Save the World,* and *Like a Tree: How Trees, Women, and Tree People Can Save the Planet* bring together the inner world of archetypes and symbols with activism in the world. Website: *www.jeanbolen.com*

## ABOUT CIRCLES

Circle Guidelines: Download from website
*www.millionthcircle.org/resources/guidelines.html*

Circle Principles: Download from website
*www.millionthcircle.org/resources/principles.html*

Circle Difficulties: *The Millionth Circle.* pp. 55–67.

## TO OUR READERS

Conari Press, an imprint of Red Wheel/Weiser, publishes books on topics ranging from spirituality, personal growth, and relationships to women's issues, parenting, and social issues. Our mission is to publish quality books that will make a difference in people's lives—how we feel about ourselves and how we relate to one another. We value integrity, compassion, and receptivity, both in the books we publish and in the way we do business.

Our readers are our most important resource, and we appreciate your input, suggestions, and ideas about what you would like to see published.

Visit our website at *www.redwheelweiser.com* to learn about our upcoming books and free downloads, and be sure to go to *www.redwheelweiser.com/newsletter/* to sign up for newsletters and exclusive offers.

You can also contact us at *info@redwheelweiser.com*.

Conari Press
an imprint of Red Wheel/Weiser, LLC
665 Third Street, Suite 400
San Francisco, CA 94107